by Char

*Southern Girls*

# COLLEGE
## Football Guide

**DISCLAIMER AND TERMS OF USE AGREEMENT**

The author and publisher of this book and the accompanying materials have used their best efforts in preparing this book. The author and publisher make no representation or warranties with respect to the accuracy, applicability, fitness, or completeness of the contents of this book. The information contained in this book is strictly for educational purposes. Therefore, if you wish to apply ideas contained in this book, you are taking full responsibility for your actions.

EVERY EFFORT HAS BEEN MADE TO ACCURATELY REPRESENT THIS PRODUCT AND IT'S POTENTIAL. EVEN THOUGH THIS INDUSTRY IS ONE OF THE FEW WHERE ONE CAN WRITE THEIR OWN CHECK IN TERMS OF EARNINGS, THERE IS NO GUARANTEE THAT YOU WILL EARN ANY MONEY USING THE TECHNIQUES AND IDEAS IN THESE MATERIALS. EXAMPLES IN THESE MATERIALS ARE NOT TO BE INTERPRETED AS A PROMISE OR GUARANTEE OF EARNINGS. EARNING POTENTIAL IS ENTIRELYDEPENDENT ON THE PERSON USING OUR PRODUCT, IDEAS AND TECHNIQUES. WE DO NOT PURPORT THIS AS A "GET RICH SCHEME."

ANY CLAIMS MADE OF ACTUAL EARNINGS OR EXAMPLES OF ACTUAL RESULTS CAN BE VERIFIED UPON REQUEST. YOUR LEVEL OF SUCCESS IN ATTAINING THE RESULTS CLAIMED IN OUR MATERIALS DEPENDS ON THE TIME YOU DEVOTE TO THE PROGRAM, IDEAS AND TECHNIQUES MENTIONED, YOUR FINANCES, KNOWLEDGE AND VARIOUS SKILLS. SINCE THESE FACTORS DIFFER ACCORDING TO INDIVIDUALS, WE CANNOT GUARANTEE YOUR SUCCESS OR INCOME LEVEL. NOR ARE WE RESPONSIBLE FOR ANY OF YOUR ACTIONS.

# DEDICATION AND THANKS

I am grateful to my family who by all rights should have refused to watch football with this irrational fan years ago.

To my niece who went for a consolation milkshake with me after the "Kick 6", my nephew who loves football as much as I, and keeps me informed on all things SEC.

To my mom, who can't watch when things go poorly, and most especially my Indiana Hoosier husband who tears up when hearing Bear Bryant's *"I ain't never been nothing but a winner"* speech on the jumbotron.

Thanks to "boys" like Roger, Danny, Conley, and Jim who answered my questions and played football with me years ago. To all the women who asked questions and gave me encouragement, I love you dearly.

And thank you to the JOX Roundtable guys at 94.5 FM in Birmingham for keeping me informed and giving females listeners some respect.

# FOREWORD

 I grew up in a small Alabama town in the 1960s. This was the type of town where, in the sogginess of a July morning, a neighbor might holler to my mama through the wooden screen door, *"Martha, you busy?"*

And in the door, she'd come to sit and have a cup of coffee, just to visit. Nothing more, no agenda other than "visiting." There was talk of the garden and vacation Bible school plans, babies, Brownie Girl Scout Day Camp, nicked knees, and grocery store sales.

My summers featured grass-stained knees and elbows, baseball cards in bicycle spokes and special days at the city pool where a quarter would buy a PayDay bar. Nights were heavy with cricket sounds and croaking frogs while I played "kick the can" with the neighbors and caught lightning bugs in mayonnaise jars that had ice pick holes poked in the lids. The little cotton window curtains in my room fluttered slightly on sultry summer nights, and a train whistle broke the heavy stillness at predictable intervals. It was a good town.

But as August drew to a close and school started back after Labor Day, things began to change. The talk and the sounds of the night became more magical than even the most stellar summer evening's offerings.

The open windows carried the beat of drums-big, loud, deep poundings accompanying the strains of marching band practice-faint but nonetheless discernible.

Football season was upon us.

The State of Alabama has never had much to brag about. On the whole, it carries a great burden of embarrassing, pockmarked events especially during the 1960s and, of course, in the years both before and after that. Still today, I shudder at the memory of the hatred and fear that marks the history of the Deep South. We didn't really know how very backward we were; we just knew what we knew. Our little town integrated without incident, and I was too young to notice anything abnormal about it at all. I didn't know the magnitude of the suffering and the price that had been paid to achieve it. I didn't know.

I believe it's this shame and horror-littered history that led us to gain such a reverence for something frivolous like football.

We craved something positive on which to hang our hats, something at which we could excel, something at which we would be called "the gold standard" rather than the brunt of the latest joke and the object of national disgust. I'm not defending it.

Alabama earned and deserved the low status bestowed upon it, but football seemed to unify our divisive culture and lead us toward better things.

In this state, you have to choose. It is a given.

Everyone makes his or her choice for one team or the other, and whole families are identified by their loyalties. When referencing

          Charlsa Perdew | NAMS, Inc.

a family, you might hear, *"Oh, sure, they're Auburn, 'always have been."* or *"Didn't you know they're Alabama?"*

Our local high school adopted a diplomatic approach when choosing a team colors and mascot. They went with Red and White (for Alabama) and a Tiger mascot (for Auburn) – a compromise no one argued against.

Friday nights, we sat under my dad's Army blanket on cold concrete bleacher seats, sipping hot chocolate from glass Thermos bottles and cheering for our Tigers. We knew the names of all the players, where they went to church and who their folks were. They were real heroes to us, win or lose. We loved them.

A tomboy, I liked to play with the boys on our street. I loved to throw the football and pretend that the game was accessible to the likes of me, a girl… My daddy loved football, and I loved my daddy. My mama grew up an Alabama fan, so we were Alabama fans as a family – it was part of our identity.

I was about 6 years old when my dad got sick. He died when I was 10. Mama moved my sister and me to a new house with a yard full of pine trees that always needed raking in the fall. We'd set up the transistor radio, leaning against a tree on those autumn Saturday afternoons and listen to Alabama football games while we piled up and burned that pine straw. I can still hear the sounds, even now – the crowd and the play-by-play announcer that brought the game to life for us.

Sunday mornings at church were glorified or tainted by the win or loss of the day before. And if the ultimate game of the year — Alabama vs. Auburn — had been played the day before, children and adults alike happily anticipated or dreaded those few moments before Sunday School when they would gloat or have to eat crow over the game's outcome. Actually, it's still that way today.

This was the pond in which I swam, and it will forever impact me, no matter where I live, work or travel. I will always be an Alabama fan, and I'll always watch for scores on football Saturdays.

As a young adult, I moved away to the big city of Atlanta, Georgia.

My team wasn't doing well during those years. I learned that any outward response to the jabs of colleagues was an incentive for them to continue the taunts. So, in the heart of Bulldog and Yellow Jacket country, I became a closeted Bama fan. I rooted for the Braves and the Hawks and went to their games, but for 20 years or more, I held back my enthusiasm for football.

And then, I moved back to Alabama.

I immediately headed to the DMV to purchase an Alabama vanity license plate and renewed my season ticket application. It wasn't long before I felt that familiar loyalty. Everywhere I looked there were Alabama hats, signs, t-shirts and bumper stickers.

It sure felt good.

The team? Well, it wasn't so great, actually. We were under NCAA sanctions and restrictions involving scholarship reductions and probationary rules. The once mighty program was a shell of itself. We waited as time ticked by.

Turns out, it was worth the wait: Celebrated former national championship winning coach Nick Saban joined us.

It felt like we had been issued a doomsday reprieve! We stopped saying, "remember when?" and looked toward the future. You really have to be a fan to understand how this coach's presence fostered a spell of renewed hope for a large group of people.

I got an idea from the movie **Julie & Julia** to begin blogging on a subject about which I was passionate — football.

Women in the south love football but as a whole, they know very little about the game itself. I decided to write a blog to teach women about college football. Followers asked questions, and I answered. If they asked something I didn't know, I did the research, and I asked questions of my friends who had played college football.

Eventually, I was asked to do a workshop for a large group. So, I assembled a PowerPoint presentation and set my fees. Local radio featured the blog on their website, and sports talk personalities took my calls on air.

Week by week, the blog grew, and information I assembled became the core of this book. I continue to update it to reflect the changes in rules and systems.

I am a small-town girl who grew up, returned to her roots and found a way to share something novel and fun.

I know that somewhere this season, a woman's increased football knowledge might just make her feel empowered in this male dominated world of football. More importantly, she might enjoy this past time that consumes southern culture, a little more, because she's better informed.

I hope you enjoy **Southern Girls College Football Guide**. Let me know by commenting on our Facebook Page or my Twitter feed.

*Charlsa Taul Perdew*

Charlsa Perdew | NAMS, Inc.

# ABOUT THE AUTHOR

Even though football is her first love, Charlsa Taul Perdew did have another love: music.

She served as a vocal music educator in metropolitan Atlanta for more than 15 years and was Adjunct Professor of Music at Georgia State University. Charlsa holds Master's Degrees in Education and Vocal Performance from the Universities of Alabama and Georgia State.

Employed by the Atlanta Opera for thirteen seasons, she twice served as mezzo soprano soloist with Atlanta Opera Studio. Via Atlanta Opera's Artist/Mentor Program she wrote curriculum guides for music camps at Atlanta's FOX THEATRE.

Charlsa directed eight State Champion vocal ensembles and was named Teacher of the Year at the Cobb County Center for Excellence in the Performing Arts. Choirs under her direction have performed at Carnegie Hall and Westminster Abby and have been featured by SHAWNEE PRESS.

Currently, Charlsa maintains a private vocal studio and lives with her husband, David in North Alabama. Her passion and love for college football led her to write *Southern Girls College Football Guide.*

Follow her on Facebook at ChuckLuvs.com/SGCFB and on Twitter at Twitter.com/charlsat.

# TABLE OF CONTENTS

      Charlsa Perdew | NAMS, Inc.

# Southern Girls

# COLLEGE

## Football Guide

# LET'S KICK IT OFF LADIES

A recent survey reveals that men across the country believe Southern women to be well informed on the topic of college football. Just how informed are we in reality? Men never REALLY talk to us about football, do they? You know they don't. But they do talk a lot about it in front of us, and the fact is most men expect us to be downright ignorant on the subject.

So, let's talk about it here. Let's ask our questions and get some answers.

We'll cover the basics and make a slight venture into the more complex. As a unified front - the "washed and the unwashed" alike, we shall face college football season as informed, literate women. We are Southern Girls who know their football. We will all relish the moment when the menfolk sit straight up in their recliners, turn their heads our way and say, "Hey, how'd you know that?"

Are you with me?

Charlsa Taul Perdew
Twitter: @charlsat
Facebook Page: http://ChuckLuvs.com/SGCFB
SouthernGirlsCollegeFootballGuide.com

Chapter 1

# WHO WE ARE

If you are wondering about the definition of girls, don't give it another thought. I use the term quite loosely here. If you are female, you qualify. If you're male, we welcome you as well.

I figure that folks reading this book will fall into 3 categories, but don't be hurt if one doesn't fit you exactly.

## Category 1:

This category includes girls who grew up watching high school and college football. They've known the game for so long that they can't remember not knowing and enjoying football. As a Category 1, you will remember going to games as a girl with your parents... sitting under a blanket, sipping hot chocolate while the hometown boys played their hearts out for their school. You recognized them when you saw them on the street in their letter jackets; you knew their folks and where they went to church; they were a part of your home and local culture, and they were your friends.

On Saturday mornings, you and the family got your chores out of the way, so you could gather around the TV or radio for your favorite college team's game. If you weren't near a TV, your radio blasted the familiar sound of your team's play-by-play announcer whose voice was like honey on a biscuit as long as your team was winning.

When losing, he made you feel like a whole nation of people was disappointed right along with you. As a teen, you played football with your friends—male and female at one of their homes on Sunday afternoon. The game always ended in time for everyone to get cleaned up for Sunday night church.

You loved that college team, and if you made it your Alma Mater, your loyalty was cemented for life. No man, marriage, professional advancement or move out of State will sway your allegiance.

Through good years or down years, there's no doubt that you are a fan.

## Category 2:

This one is probably more common. It is for girls who never really paid attention to the *details* of the game. They loved the social atmosphere of high school and college football and the excitement that was involved.

I'll bet you meant to and were going to, but you just never got around to understanding what was going on. If you are reading this, then you've probably decided you'd like to be able to follow a game, and you'd enjoy throwing around some words like linebacker, offensive linemen, shut-down corner and holding penalty.

Some of you might want to go even further and understand what the refs are saying with all those hand signal thingies. Our really serious girls might like to make the sort of intelligent comments during the games that make the men take their hands out of the snack mix, put down their drinks and turn to look their way in amazement!

Doesn't that thought just make you smile? I can tell you that it's loads of fun!

## Category 3:

The 3rd category is for you girls who are ready to sincerely enjoy this college football season. Year after year you've been on the periphery while everybody you knew seemed enthralled with football from August to January. Not only was it *not fun*, but it was also downright demoralizing to realize that for 14 plus weeks you were going to have to endure something totally baffling. AND you'd be preparing snacks and cleaning up after the guests that had come over to watch the game.

*"This year,"* you decided, *"I will join in and be a part of this, even if it kills me."* Don't worry; it won't. Once you have a little knowledge, you will find that College Football isn't so bad after all. You might even get the chance to do a little pay-back by yelling and trashing up someone else's home this season. And, if this opportunity presents itself, you'd be foolish to pass it up!

# WHY READ THIS BOOK

## Category 1 Girls:

You need to read this book because, like it or not, the sports writers, announcers and TV folks ALL cater to men and they make the assumption that the listener understands the latest terms and lingo.

In this book, you'll read intelligent talk about the game and rules, and you'll get concise definitions. No one here will *roll their eyes* when giving simple explanations.

This little book is designed to make football season more enjoyable for you.

## Categories 2 and 3 Girls:

You will want to read this book because it will help build your football knowledge. You won't get any patronizing answers here, and you'll gain a base knowledge that will turn this college football season into a more pleasant and positive experience for you.

Set a goal for yourself. What do you want to know?

## For All:

Here we can all find a little relief for our football frustrations because *Knowledge is Power*. Who knows? Sports Center may become your go-to news channel!

Charlsa Perdew | NAMS, Inc.

Chapter 2

# STARTING FROM SCRATCH

## OFFENSE has the ball; the DEFENSE doesn't...

Okay, here we go. Each team has a goal line to defend. It's actually marked as the "0" yard line. The DEFENSE has the objective of keeping the team who has the ball (the OFFENSE) from moving the ball across the goal line they are defending. Stop and think about that for a minute. Take a look at a picture of a football field; it will help.

## KICK OFFS QUARTERS AND SUCH

At the beginning of the game, representative players from each team called Team Captains meet with the Officials at mid-field at the 50-yard line for a **coin toss.**

The toss determines which team will kick the ball and which team will receive the ball to start the game. Just to be fair, this is reversed for the second half of play. The team that wins the coin toss gets to pick whether they will receive or **kick** and which end of the field they'd like to defend.

Why wouldn't they ALWAYS choose to receive? Well, they might want to kick so that they can receive at the beginning of the 2nd half.

The college game is divided into four 15-minute **quarters**. At the end of each quarter, the teams switch the end of the field they will defend. A 20-minute **halftime** break lies between the second and third quarters. During halftime, you'll see the bands play if you are at the game. If you are watching from home, you'll almost never see the bands. *It's too bad because they have been practicing really hard.*

Each team has 11 players on the field. The Offense often will huddle-up in a bunch prior to each play to discuss which play to run. Some teams use what they call a *"hurry-up offense"* that skips the huddle. This is designed to catch the Defense off its guard to prevent the Defense from substituting fresh players onto the field. This also happens when game time is running short, and the Offense needs another score.

Players must stay on their side of the line of **scrimmage** (an imaginary line extending from where the ball is placed) until the ball is **snapped** by the Center.

Traditionally, the Quarterback will then pass the ball, run with it himself, or hand it off to another player while the Defense tries to stop the play from progressing.

## Kick Offs

At the game's beginning, after halftime, and after every score, there is a kick-off. The ball is placed on a little holder (called a tee) on the 35-yard line. Remember, the coin toss determines which team kicks off at the beginning of the game, and reverses this after halftime.

After any kind of score, the team that scored the points will do the kicking (except in the case of a SAFETY. More later on that). This takes place from the 35-yard line of the kicking team. The kicker kicks the ball down the field toward the receiving team. A player on that team catches it.

He might decide to raise his hand prior to catching it to signal a **fair catch** (the play stops there, and he can't be tackled). Or, he might catch the ball and run with it toward the other team's goal line.

If the kicker kicks the ball into the end zone, without any player touching it, it is called a **touchback**, and the play then begins from the 25-yard line. Furthermore, if the ball is caught in the end zone, the player may kneel down with the ball to signal a **touchback** which also means that play will begin from the 25-yard line.

## Penalties

The team which has been fouled is allowed to decide whether to accept or decline the penalty. They will accept the penalty if it benefits them and decline if they prefer the results of the play. Sometimes both teams are penalized on the same play. The penalties are offsetting, and neither is assessed a loss of yardage.

It's like 2 wrongs make a right.

More about penalties is discussed later, but let's just say that common penalties are 5, 10 and 15 yards. The maximum penalty is half the distance to the goal, so if the Offense is 5 yards from the goal and the Defense receives a penalty of 5 yards, then the penalty is reduced to 2 ½ yards.

## The CLOCK

The **game clock** stops frequently throughout the game. It stops in between downs, for incomplete passes or when a player goes out of bounds with the ball. The clock is also stopped briefly prior to each first down play to allow the folks that hold the yard marker chains to move the 10-yard length chain to the new spot.

This new spot shows the yard line to which the team must progress for a new set of 4 downs. The clock also stops of course, in the event of an injury.

Each team has 3 **timeouts** per half of play which can be used at any time. This stops the clock as well.

Stopping the clock with incomplete passes and running the ball out of bounds is often done in the last couple of minutes of the game by the Offense to save time and increase their chance to score. Now, we also have **TV timeouts**. These seem to be numerous and last a LONG time.

So, you can see that stopping the clock for all these particular reasons might cause a game of four 15-minute quarters to last up to 4 hours!

# YARD LINES

The middle of the field is marked as the **50-yard line**. On either side of the 50, the yard lines decrease in 5-yard increments to the 0-yard line otherwise known as the **Goal Line**. So, the whole field is a total of 100 yards - from 0 to 50 at one end, and 0 to 50 at the other. Take a look at a field. It'll make perfect sense.

      Charlsa Perdew | NAMS, Inc.

## The "Down" deal

The Offense has 4 tries to move the ball 10 yards. Each try is called a **down**. They may throw the ball (called a **pass**) or **run** with it.

**First Down** means the team has moved the ball forward 10 yards (remember, they get 4 tries at this) and they get a gift: *Four more DOWNS to try it all again.* In this way, they move the ball down the field and toward their opponent's goal line to attempt to score points.

If a team does NOT make the first down in three tries, they usually decide to **punt** ( a type of kick) the ball as far as possible in the other direction (away from their goal line) on their 4th down. This is most often done when things aren't going so well for the Offense, and they just can't seem to move the ball the 10 yards they need. This is called, *punting on 4th down.* If the Punter kicks the ball past the Goal Line into the End Zone, the ball is automatically moved out to the 25-yard line where the other teams take possession.

Sometimes, the Offense will actually decide to go for it on 4th down. If they make it past the First Down marker, it's all good, and they get another series of 4 downs. But if they don't make it, the other team gets to take possession of the ball right there, where the Offense landed.

You can understand why a team would not want to take the risk, especially if they are still really close to their own goal line. In that situation, they would use their Punter to send it way down the field so the other team would have a long, long way to go in order to score.

The announcers on radio and TV are usually good at keeping track and telling us how much yardage was achieved on each down. For example, they might say *"It's 2nd and 4."* This means that the Offense went 6 yards (10-6=4) on their 1st down and now, it is 2nd down, and they need 4 more yards to reach the First Down Marker.

This is also displayed on the scoreboards at games or at the bottom or top of your TV screen.

# SCORING

## Touchdown

Teams score 6 points when they carry the ball, or pass and catch it, past the other team's goal line. This is a TOUCHDOWN. The rule is that the ball has to break the *imaginary* plane above the Zero-yard line or Goal line.

You'll see players trying to hold the ball out in front of them in order to break that plane. Also, you'll see plays designed to allow the player to leap over a huge pile of scuffling and pushing men to get the ball across the line.

     Charlsa Perdew | NAMS, Inc.

## How to Impress Your Football Friends:

Watch for yourself and feel free to make comments about your view of the replay, like *"I just don't think the ball broke the plane before his knee came down!"*

When it's a little iffy as to whether the ball went across the line before the player's knee touched the ground, a replay review is done by the Officials. They will look at it from all angles to determine the truth. However, this method is not fool proof; officials can miss a call even with the aid of video evidence.

## P.A.T. (Point after Touchdown)

After each touchdown, the scoring team gets a chance to kick the ball through the arms of the goal post. This counts for 1 point and is called a P.A.T. (point after touchdown).

## How to Impress Your Football Friends:

To sound like you are knowledgeable, just turn your head during the kick to speak to someone, THEN when you turn back around ask aloud, *"Did he get the P. A. T.?" (be careful to spell this out, don't say it like a person's name...it'll give you away)*

On rather rare occasions, a team may elect to **go for** 2 after a touchdown. This means that the team decides not to kick the P.A.T., but will run *one play* to see if they can get it across the Goal line. They get 2 points if they do a so-called a **2-Point Conversion.**

## Field Goal

**Field goals** count 3 points. A player kicks the ball (while a teammate holds it steady) through the goal posts...usually on a 4th Down. If he kicks it through the goal posts, it's good for 3 points, but if he misses, the other team gets the ball.

## Safety

These are pretty unusual, but they are good for 2 points. This means the Offense is getting creamed, and the Defensive team actually tackles the ball carrier behind the Offense's goal line.

It's a sort of demoralizing thing for the Offense, but the Defense gets the 2 points. (I know, that really is hard to explain, but clear when you see it happen). To make matters even worse, the Defense NOW gets the ball as well as the 2 points! Thus, the demoralizing nature of the **Safety**.

## Defense

The job of the **Defense** put simply, is to thwart the attempts of the Offense to move the ball down the field to score. They tackle the ball carrier, harass the Quarterback, try to keep the passes from being caught and the kicks from getting off the ground.

 Charlsa Perdew | NAMS, Inc.

The **Defense** wants the **Offense** to fail to make **First Downs** and be forced to **Punt**. They try to pull the ball from Offensive player's hands, knock it loose during passing or running plays, and block kicks by running like mad at the kicker or punter.

The **Defense** can take on many formations, and they can adjust and move about as they see what play the Offense has up their sleeve.

A good defensive football play is a hallmark of Southern football. We will learn a bit more about this later on.

Chapter 3

# PLAYER POSITIONS

## (Generally speaking)

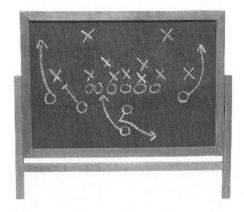

There are so many different Player Positions because the game of football is adaptive. Coaches get new ideas and decide to try some of them. When someone develops a Defense that "can't be stopped," there will likely be an Offensive scheme introduced to counter it. Through the years these adaptations have surfaced, and for every adaptation, another adjustment emerges. I'm just trying to say that it is hard to cover it all.

The names for positions on **Offense** and, especially, on **Defense**, seem to change from play to play and year to year as well. So, I am covering this in real generalities here, and I hope that these basics will help lay a little ground work from which to start.

All this change is frustrating for me, a girl who grew up on the Offensive play style known as the *Wishbone*. For years, I was disgusted as team after team went to the *"I Formation."* I understood the "wishbone" plays, and I was loathed to leave the familiar.

Occasionally we will hear an announcer mention that a play *"hearkens back to the ol' wishbone style."*

I perk up like my name had just been called at the Fulton County DMV! However, they don't *"hearken"* all that much if you ask me.

# OFFENSE

### Quarterback (QB)

The Quarterback (QB), the key player, receives the ball from the Center (C) under normal circumstances. The C snaps (quickly gives) the ball to the QB at the QB's **signal** to do so. The signal may be shouted or visual.

QB's also determine each play either on their own or by receiving a message from the coaches on the sideline. QB's may run with the ball, pass it or hand it off to another player. They must remember tons of **plays** and also be able to read the schemes of the Defense before making decisions about throwing or running, etc. So, they need to be smart and quick as well as enthusiastic leaders and motivators.

Being cute is nice, too.

Actually, they usually ARE cute. I can think of only a couple of exceptions, but it wouldn't be nice to mention names.

## Center (C)

This guy is easily identified as he crouches over the ball in a very unflattering pose.

The C gives the ball quickly to the QB at a predetermined signal and then blocks the oncoming Defensive linemen who are headed his way. The C has to be able to "read" defensive schemes and communicate these with team members in a matter of seconds.

This is usually a BIG guy, with a quick mind and ability to remain composed in the face of scary oncoming traffic. I think nerves of steel would be required to play this position because the *C knows* that he will be hit hard on most every play.

## Running back (RB)

These players are lined up behind the Offensive line and run with the football after receiving it from the QB or the C. They can be called **tailbacks, halfbacks, scat-backs, wingbacks** and so forth and they line up behind the Offensive line somewhere in the backfield. They should be fast, sturdy and able to dart about, elusively.

## Fullback (FB)

Fullbacks (also not on Offensive line) can be ball carriers, or they may function as blockers. They are usually stockier than other "backs" and are often called upon for short yardage plays where they use their strong legs to bulldoze their way with the ball.

## Guards- Left and Right (LG, RG)

These are members of the Offensive line on each side of the C. They block or protect (guard) the **QB** or other ball carriers. They are not ball carriers. *(There used to be a deodorant called, "Right Guard"...is that still around?)*

## Tackles-Left and Right (LT, RT)

**Tackles** are the outermost members on the standard Offensive line (on either side of the L and R Guards), 2 player positions down from the Center in typical formations. Oddly, they don't really "tackle" ...they block. Many football terms make no sense at all.

## Tight End (TE)

This player lines up next to the outside edge of the Tackles. They run pass routes to catch the ball or may be blockers on a play. It's nice if they are tall and strong.

## Wide receiver (WR)

They usually get their name because of where they line up on Offense. *Wide* or separate from the **down lineman** (men on the line with 1 or both hands down on the ground, i.e., the word *down*). There may be 2-4 Wide Receivers, depending on the Offensive scheme. The word *receiver* means they are running particular patterns on the field and are supposed to catch the ball when thrown to them by the QB.

# DEFENSE

**Note:** *Names for defensive player Positions vary with the particular defensive schemes today.*

**Down Linemen** are players on the *line of scrimmage* who have one or both of their hands on the ground at the beginning of the play.

## Nose Guard (NG)

This player lines up directly across from the C. At the snap of the ball, he charges in an attempt to reach the ball carrier.

## Defensive Tackles (DT)

Mostly, these guys stay in their positions on the interior of the Defensive line and try to stop a runner who has the ball. Also, they may break through to the QB or backfield. They actually TACKLE. *(Finally, something that makes perfect sense!)*

## Defensive Ends (DE)

Yep, you guessed it...they are on the END of the Defensive line as a rule. They are assigned to break through blocking to get into the Offensive back field and tackle the ball carrier. However, if the play goes to the outside, they're supposed to *herd* the ball carrier off to the sideline or into other Defensive folks on their team.

## Cornerbacks (CB)

These guys line up to the *wide* side, where they can cover **WR's** who are running routes to catch passes. Their job is to keep the receiver from catching the pass or better yet, intercepting it themselves!

## Linebackers (LB)

They line up behind the defensive line where the NG, DT's and DE's are. Different schemes require different numbers of LB's and may call them something else (sorry). They must be great at pursuit, tackling and *reading* how a play is going to unfold. They defend the short pass and the running plays. Typically, there are 3 or 4 LB's, and they all get a different nickname because of their particular position or assignment. Some nicknames may be, *Sam, Mike, Will, or Jack. By the way, I'm not kidding here.*

## Safety/Safeties (S)

Safeties line up behind the LB's, further away from the line of scrimmage (called the **Secondary**) than the other defenders. Their name indicates their role as they are to stop the ball carrier if the pass is caught or a long run is in progress. There are 2 types of Safeties: **Free** and **Strong**.

Remember: this is a POSITION, not to be confused with the point scoring term, *safety*.

The Free Safety plays downfield and is responsible for stopping the long pass. The Strong Safety is more responsible for the mid-field passes.

(These definitions are huge generalizations.)

They have to have the speed of a Wide Receiver and the "go-getter" mentality of a Linebacker.

# A GENERIC LINEUP OF OFFENSE AND DEFENSE

## DEFENSE

```
                 S            S

          LB    LB                LB

     CB            DE   DT   NG   DT   DE
```

## OFFENSE

```
     WR      TE   LT   LG   C     RG    RT     WR

                           QB

                      FB   RB
```

Chapter 4

# HOW DID YOU KNOW THAT WAS A PENALTY?

The men wearing the black and white stripes and white britches are called **Officials**. There are 8 of them in Division 1 College football, and each one has a special *title* although we often call all of them *refs*. (Referee, Umpire, Head Linesman, Line Judge, Back Judge, Side Judge, Center Judge and Field Judge).

These guys are important and do all sorts of things to make the game go smoothly.

They often lose popularity by throwing their little yellow cloths. Folks call these **flags** and the terminology used is *"There is a flag on the play."*

When officials pull a yellow flag out of their pocket, they are signaling that someone has broken a rule and committed a **foul**. (There are LOTS of rules.)

The officials get close together and discuss what they saw and what should be done. A **penalty** is a punishment for the **foul**. The team being punished gives up 5, 10 or even 15 yards.

There can be more than one penalty on a given play which can create a bunch of confusion.

By the way, the officials use hand signals for all these fouls and penalties.

# COMMON PENALTIES

**Delay of game** – this means the **Offense** took too much time to get lined up and get the ball in the hands of the quarterback. (FYI: the center squats down over the ball and snaps it back into the hands of the quarterback.) This is a 5-yard penalty.

## How to Impress Your Football Friends:

You might want to learn some of the hand signals so you can shout out loud before anyone else. Show your approval or disgust with comments like, *"It's about time you called "holding!"* or *"Come on, ref! Intentional grounding?"*

**Encroachment / Off-sides** - a Defensive player moved across the yard line where the ball is sitting (line of scrimmage) and makes contact with an Offensive player. If he gets back BEFORE the snap without bumping any Offensive player, it's okay; but if not, the Defense is penalized 5 yards.

**False Start** - The Offense moves across the year line where the ball is sitting before the Center snaps the ball. This is called **a false-start,** and it carries a 5-yard penalty as well. Additionally, any of the Offensive line players with their hands on the ground can't even flinch before the ball is snapped. I bet that it's hard to hold still when you are staring at a bunch of huge Defensive linemen who are about to come running full-speed in your direction!

**Holding** – an Offensive lineman (the guy who lines up on the line of scrimmage or the line where the ball sits) uses his hands to keep a Defensive player from getting away and going after the ball. It's a 10-yard penalty.

**Pass Interference** - this is called if there is grabbing, tackling, or messing with the arms of someone trying to catch the pass while it's in the air. Mostly this is called on the Defense because he must wait until the ball arrives to disrupt the pass or even catch it himself (an interception).

This penalty is 15 yards, and a first down is awarded to the non-offending team. Big penalty.

(I should tell you that on rare occasions, Offensive pass interference is called).

**Clipping, Chop Block, Block in the Back** – this is hitting the player from behind. These illegal blocks are dangerous because the player doesn't see what's coming and can be injured badly. It's a 10-yard penalty.

# REALLY SERIOUS PENALTIES...15 YARDS

**Unnecessary roughness, roughing the passer or the kicker** – involves hitting the player after the play is over, the player no longer has the ball, or the player is out of bounds.

As implied, this foul is called when a player purposely tries to inflict injury beyond a normal level of aggression. Incidentally, the normal level of aggression can be pretty intense.

**Facemask** – grabbing another player's facemask or helmet as you might guess, could cause serious neck or head injury when a player is running at full tilt.

**Unsportsmanlike conduct or personal foul** – Can cover a lot of bad behavior including temper tantrums, punching or hitting, arguing with an official or referee, helmet to helmet contact, taunting, over celebrating a positive play, etc. Coaches can get in trouble for acting-up as well.

**Targeting** – A player leads with his head when tackling or blocking a defenseless player and makes contact with the other player's head or helmet. This can carry a 15-yard penalty or ejection from the game if it is determined blatant.

**Horse-collar** – this is a tackle that involves a Defensive player grabbing the ball carrier's shoulder pads to bring him down.

There are several websites that discuss and show pictures of Official's Hand Signals. The sacred NCAA site lists all the rules… and I mean ALL of them.

Don't go searching unless you have some extra time on your hands.

Chapter 5

# ANYBODY WANT TO TRANSLATE?

When watching football or listening to sports commentators, you'll notice that the announcer folks have a kind of lingo that contains catchy little words and phrases. These guys assume that they need no explanation.

Here are some explanations for these words and phrases, just in case you think they DO require explaining.

**Ju-Co (pronounced Joo-coh)** - The player is a transfer from a Junior College

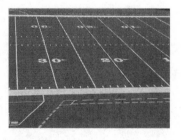

**Hash marks** – these are two rows of short lines near the middle of the football field, parallel to the side lines.

The officials set the ball on or between the hash marks before the play starts. So, if the ball is downed in between a hash mark and the nearest sideline, it is reset on the hash mark for the next play.

(In other words, they are markers that help the officials when setting the ball down for the next play)

**BCS** – This is an acronym for Bowl Championship Series. Although we no longer have this method of finding a champion, you may still hear all sorts of folks on TV and Radio mention it. We now have a playoff system instead.

**Four TEAM PLAY-OFFS** - In a nutshell, this is a system of selecting the nation's best 4 teams to play in end-of-the-year semi-finals. The 2 winners of the semi-final games will play in the National Championship Game which determines the National Champion. A committee has been appointed to determine these 4 teams.

I wouldn't want to be on that committee.

**Bowl Games** – End of year games designed to be big time money makers for the sponsors of the bowl. They shamelessly name the bowl for the corporate sponsor, and some of them are downright funny. The **New Year's 6 Bowls** feature top ranked teams in the big-name bowls.

## How to Impress Your Football Friends:

An intelligent question to pose on this topic might be something like, "What effect do you think the Play Off system has had on the success of Bowl Games?" If asked for your opinion, just say "I think I'll wait to see how it plays out this season."

**Wildcat formation (*also known as a Wild hog*)** – This is a type of play used by the Offense that Arkansas helped popularize. It can be explained in great detail, but let's just say that the Offense lines up in an unbalanced-looking formation and a running back takes the snap from Center rather than the Quarterback. After the snap, a variety of options are available, including a pass by the running back and a sweep run behind some blockers.

## How to Impress Your Football Friends:

Appear informed and say, *"Wow! Barry Sanders all over again!"*

**Rushing Yards** – This is totally easy to understand. Aren't you glad? It just means the number of yards the team or a player accumulates on running plays, i.e., yards gained without passing the ball.

This is sometimes called yards on the ground. You might hear, *"We held them to 60 yards rushing."* That means that the Defense kept the other team's Offense from running the ball well.

Also, individual players might be lauded for their total rushing yards because they racked up a lot of them. For example, in 1988 Barry Sanders had 2628 total yards rushing in one season.

**Spread Offense** - The object of the spread Offense is to open up/spread out the Offense's formation so that the Defense is forced to spread itself thin across the field to cover (stay with) everyone. The Quarterback stands back away from the Center (shotgun formation), and they can have as many as 5 receivers spread out. There are several forms of this Offense and Defenses are learning more all the time about how to best defend against it.

**Betting terms: I'll take Miami and the points; Texas -14, Miami +14** – I think this is just a weird way to say it. It means that the predictions have Texas beating Miami by more points than you think they'll be able to make. You still think Miami is going to lose, but not by as many "points" as the betting predictions.

*"Texas -14"* means that they are supposed to beat Miami by 14 points. *"Miami + 14"* means that they will lose by 14 or more. See why I said it was a weird way to put it? **A PUSH** means that there is no real winner or loser predicted in terms of the wagering community. To college football fans, there is never a case where there is no *real* winner.

**Sack** – This just means that the Defense broke through the Offensive blockers and tackled the Quarterback behind the line of scrimmage resulting in a loss of yardage.

**Clock Management** – This is usually mentioned during the latter part of the 1st half or in the closing minutes of the game. It speaks of the Offense using their timeouts, plays without a huddle, and plays that stop the Game Clock in a way that provides for more opportunity to score to win OR to keep the other team from getting the ball again.

**Pump Fake** – Another easy one…the Quarterback moves his arm in a motion that looks like he's throwing the ball, but holds on to it. This is designed to *fake out* the Defense and make them commit to covering a receiver that's not going to be the QB's target.

**Deep at that position** – In this context, it simply means that the team has several players who play the position well.

This is great because the players can be taken in and out of play to rest and if someone is injured, a replacement is prepared to go into the game.

**Draw Play** – the **QB** moves backward as if to pass, in order to draw the Defense toward him to create more room for the run.

This works best I believe if the Defense is known to blitz or be really keen on a strong pass rush.

**Fleaflicker** – the **QB** hands the ball off to a player in the backfield who then passes the ball to an eligible receiver down the field.

**Tackle Box** - This is the imaginary area on the Defensive side of the ball, directly opposite the Offensive linemen and about 5 yards deep. Actually, it is just across from where the two Offensive Tackles line up prior to the snap.

Within the tackle box is where most running plays operate. The Defense tries to stop the run before it gets past this box and down the field for big yardage.

**The Bobcat** - Refer to the previous explanation of the wildcat or wild hog Offensive play. On this one, the **QB** not only isn't behind **Center**, but he is also actually off the field and standing on the sidelines. He is not in the play at all!

**Shut down corner** – A Corner Back is a Defensive player. A shutdown Corner means that this Defensive player just rarely lets the Offensive guy he covers get by him or catch a pass for any yardage.

**Dive Play** –This is very common as far as running plays go in football. Usually, it is used for short yardage or maybe goal line Offense. A running back takes the ball (via handoff as a rule) and dives into the center of the line for short yardage.

There are variations on this of course, including faking the dive play to get the Defense to focus on the wrong man which in turn, allows the QB to throw downfield (a play action pass).

Charlsa Perdew | NAMS, Inc.

Chapter 6

# THE BEST OFFENSE IS A GOOD DEFENSE...

## DEFENSIVE PASS COVERAGE

Let's visit some of the Defensive pass coverage terms that we hear about. There are a couple of coverage types that we can discuss here, in a very, very general way. Maybe that will help us a bit.

The two main categories for pass coverage are:

**Man-to-Man** – Each Offensive receiver is covered by a Defensive back or linebacker.

**Zone** – Here, Defensive players have an area or zone of the field to cover.

Sometimes we hear the announcers say things like, *"cover 1"* or *"cover 2"* or even *"cover 0"*.

**Cover 0** is just a case of plain ol' **man-to-man** coverage with no help from the safeties. Often, this accompanies a blitz play by the Defense where at least 5 men cross the line of scrimmage.

**Cover 1** is man-to-man coverage with one safety helping out with downfield pass coverage.

**Cover 2** can be Zone Coverage or Man-to-Man.

**Cover 2 Zone** has the 2 safeties play deep, and each covers their area of the field.

**Cover 2 Man** is where the safeties cover a specific receiver as do other backs and linebackers.

**Cover 3 Zone** is where the Strong Safety/Cornerback helps the Safeties and the three of them divide the field into thirds (instead of half).

**Cover 4 Zone** is where both Cornerbacks join the Safeties, and they divide the field coverage with each taking a fourth.

    Charlsa Perdew | NAMS, Inc.

Chapter 7

# WHAT'S ALL THIS TALK ABOUT GUNS?

If you listen closely to announcers, you'll hear terminology that makes it sound like the Wild West has been revived in NCAA football. Let's see if we can explore what the commentators mean when they refer to Offensive formations like the SHOTGUN, the PISTOL, the GUN, the BOOTLEG and (excuse me for this one) the NAKED BOOTLEG. So here we go with the best explanations I can come up with — from a Southern Girls point of view, that is!

## The Shotgun

This Offensive scheme is not new. It's been around for a long time; some say all the way back to the days of Knute Rockne and the Fighting Irish. I apologize to y'all for mentioning that Indiana team.

Seven men line up on the line of scrimmage (the Center and 3 on each side of him). About 7 yards behind the Center, the Quarterback lines up. The Quarterback might have another back on one OR both sides of him, and there again, he might be the only one in the backfield with the rest of the backs spread out as receivers.

It is said to be like a shotgun in that receivers are sort of *sprayed* about the field in the way a shotgun sprays ammunition. Others say the formation itself looks like a shotgun...I don't see it, but 'could be.

An advantage of the shotgun is that since the QB is further back from the line of scrimmage, he has some extra seconds to look for receivers and to make decisions before the Defense comes barreling in toward him.

Disadvantages exist too, in that the Defense can usually predict a pass play is coming when they see this formation. Also, the Center has to snap the ball further back thus increasing the risk of a snap that isn't on target.

Announcers sometimes just call it the GUN for short.

## The Pistol

This seems to be just a variation on the shotgun. The QB lines up a little closer to the Center—maybe 5 yards back, rather than 7. Then another back lines up 2-3 yards behind the QB. Often, this formation is run with 3 Wide Receivers (they line up standing wide apart from the others).

The PISTOL gives the option of running or passing, depending on what the QB sees the Defense is planning to do. This one has a lot of options for short passes or reverses or counter runs.

## The Bootleg

In the bootleg, the QB pretends (fakes) a hand-off to one of the backs so that the Defensive players will be drawn away from the real ball carrier. Then the QB moves in the OPPOSITE direction to either pass or run the ball himself. He does this with the blocking protection of a few linemen, while the rest of the linemen are faking blocking for the pretend ball carrier. To be successful, the QB and the running back have to be good actors and draw the Defense to the wrong player.

Furthermore, if the QB does this whole fake job and then runs to the opposite side without the protection of any linemen, it is called the NAKED BOOTLEG -obviously, because the QB is left "naked," without any blocking coverage. In this case, the QB is banking on his acting skills being *really* good.

Chapter 8

# YOU'RE KIDDING RIGHT?

## NUMBERS GAME

One of my favorite southern female football fans asked a great question about football player's *numbers*. She had been trying to soak up the jargon and the rules and was feeling empowered. Without warning however, she felt the ol' familiar *"This is hopeless!"* feeling return as she realized that two different players on her team had the same number on their jerseys.

Practically speaking, you can see why there is a problem with today's large college rosters. There are only 99 numbers, and they simply run out of numbers. So, they have to duplicate. Usually, this involves giving the same number to a player on Defense and then, to another that plays only Offense.

Therefore, the players aren't on the field at the same time. No matter to me though, 'cause I'm confused anyway. This is especially true if one of the duplicate numbered players is a prominent one and I know him by name when I see his number.

I have said aloud at a game, *"Hey, why is JJ playing on Defense?"* A student who sits near us at the stadium looks at me with disgust and says something like, *"that is NOT JJ, it's so and so..."* This leaves me feeling like a total loser who has not taken the time to memorize the entire roster of my team.

This kid knows all of them, it's amazing.

There are some fairly clear guidelines about numbers corresponding to positions played that the NFL utilizes. You might find these helpful. For example:

- **1 -19** are usually worn by quarterbacks, kickers and punters BUT sometimes wide receivers and Defensive Safeties and Corners will wear these as well.

- **20-49** are for running backs, cornerbacks, and safeties. (40-49 might go to tight ends if 80-89 are not available)

- **50-59** are linebackers and Offensive linemen.

- **60-79** can be worn by both the Offensive line and the Defensive line.

- **80-89** are for wide receivers and tight ends.

- **90-99** are often for linebackers and defensive linemen.

Now, some college teams adhere closely to these NFL rules, but most follow it much more loosely, and there's the rub. The one real requirement seems to be that Offensive linemen (Centers, Guards, and Tackles) that play in *ineligible* (not ball carriers) positions must wear numbers between 50-79. The lower numbers are more *in demand* and seem to be more prestigious. The 40's and 90's often go to kickers and punters because these numbers are not as in demand. I know, this is rather vague, but it's true.

There are some traditions regarding numbers worn that you may find as interesting as I do. Certain numbers may even carry superstitions.

The top *walk-on player* at Texas A&M might get the number 12, referencing their *12thMan tradition*.

At Ole Miss, the number 38 was worn by Chuck Mullins who was injured during a game and died 2 years later. The #38 was given to a Defensive player each year that exemplified Mullin's spirit of performance until it was retired in 2006.

Michigan gives great honor to the number 1.

The University of Alabama gives prestige to the number 12, which was once worn by Coach Paul "Bear" Bryant, Kenny Stabler, Joe Namath and others.

So, there it is. I think that most will agree that it is just confusing. Until I memorize the roster and each of the 110 plus player's positions, it is likely to remain so.

## A SHIRT OF A DIFFERENT COLOR

Why are they talking about a **redshirt** when their colors are orange and blue?

In college athletics, the term, *redshirt* refers to delaying or suspending a player's participation for a year. It's sort of like putting him in the freezer for a year and pulling him out to use later on, or maybe not. It's really for the purpose of developing the player before putting him in a game, and it preserves a year of eligibility for him.

Usually, an athlete has 4 years of eligibility to play college sports. If *redshirted*, the player can prolong his time with the team in order to develop more thoroughly, recover from an injury, or even due to transfer status from another school.

During the redshirt year, he may practice and take academic subjects at the university or college but may not compete.

Participating in any competitive play during the year typically disables the redshirt status. Often, we hear of *redshirt freshmen*.

When we hear that someone is a *5th-year senior*, he has been *redshirted* for one year of his college tenure.

## SPARE CHANGE

Have you noticed coaches or announcers making comments like, "That's that little dime package in action" and "Notice how the Defense is rotating back and forth between the nickel and dime?"

These are Defensive schemes.

**Nickel** – this Defensive scheme has 5 Defensive Backs (the 5th one is called the Nickel Back), 4 Down-linemen and 2 Linebackers.

**Dime** – this one has 6 Defensive Backs, 3 Down-lineman, and 1 Linebacker. The "6th" Defensive Back is also called a **Nickel Back.** So, I guess the 2 Nickel Backs would make a DIME. 5 + 5 = 10

Charlsa Perdew | NAMS, Inc.

# GUEST INTERVIEWS

## Jim Eidson, Mississippi State

Jim Eidson is a graduate of Morgan County High School in Alabama. He played college ball at Mississippi State University as a standout offensive lineman earning All-SEC honors. As the second-round draft pick to the Dallas Cowboys, he became a part of the Super Bowl XII championship team. Jim's talents and achievements took him to the NFL as a Dallas Cowboy and beyond to a successful business career. At Mississippi State, he received his Bachelor of Science degree and later completed a

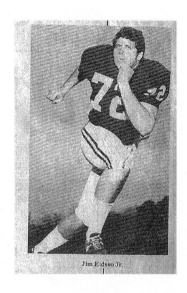
Jim Eidson Jr.

Master's Degree in Business Administration in Finance Strategy, Marketing and Business Policy at SMU. Jim is currently President of Precedent Equities, LLC., which specializes in commercial real estate and development with a Health Care focus. He is a proud father and devoted husband. He and his wife, Jana Beth make their home in Dallas, Texas

Charlsa: I know you played football for the larger portion of your young life, but at what age did you become a "starter" and where did you first play?

**Jim:** My first attempt at organized football was the summer before the 7th grade. I came to practice in my steel spiked baseball shoes. I made it without notice until about 3 plays into a scrimmage, and some of the offensive players began telling the coach that I was stepping on them with my steel cleats. The coach advised me to go home and tell my parents that I needed some football shoes. In those days, football cleats had steel tips as well, so I didn't see the big difference.

Charlsa: Did you start out in High School as an Offensive lineman?

**Jim:** I started both ways in high school, both offensive and defensive tackle.

Charlsa: The size and skill sets of linemen have changed since your college playing days. What major differences do you see from those days and the offensive linemen of today?

**Jim:** The weight difference is substantial. I played at approximately 255-265 lbs. That's about 35-40 lbs. lighter than today's norm. The most significant difference is speed. In my era, we used solo tackle sweeps and guard & tackle sweeps. We could get to the POA (Point of Attack) and turn upfield to lead the sweep play. Sweeps are very rare in today's game because the linemen are generally too big to get to the outside perimeter in the allotted time. On a straight zone blocking play, today's linemen use a form of tripod blocking with their head and hands. The use of hands was much more restrictive in my era.

Charlsa: Tell us about a "stand-out" moment as a Mississippi State Bulldog.

**Jim:** A moment that changed my life came in the spring of 1974, my sophomore year in college. I had been moved from defensive tackle and was trying to make my way to be the starter at right tackle. We had a defensive end by the name of Jimmy Webb who was All-SEC and All American at MSU. He would later be the #1 pick of the SF 49'ers in the spring of 1975. Jimmy Webb was about 6'5" and 250 lbs., and it was nearly impossible to hook block Webb on a wide play to his side of the field. If you blocked Webb, you had to earn it.

During a 100-play marathon Spring scrimmage, we ran an outside play to my side of the line. I was able to get leverage on Webb by hooking his outside shoulder with my head and inside shoulder. I continued the block and took him to the ground. As I looked up from the ground, I saw the trailing linebacker and was able to put him on the ground as well. Later, I learned that Red Hickey, former Head Coach of the 49'ers and current chief scout for the Dallas Cowboys was watching our spring scrimmage from the stands. As a result of that play, I became a marked prospect for the Dallas Cowboys.

Charlsa: As a 2$^{nd}$ round draft pick in 1976 for The Dallas Cowboys, you were certainly marked as an outstanding player. Would you tell us a bit about your experiences in the "pros"?

**Jim:** I never aspired to play pro ball. My focus was on college ball, as a means of paying my way through college. Following my senior season in college, I began receiving invitations to several post-season games. I was confident that I could compete at the next level. In April of 1976, the Cowboys selected me in the 2$^{nd}$ round of the NFL draft. Following college, I moved to Dallas to begin working out and learning the Cowboy system. Pro ball is a very different experience than you might think. It is all about the highest levels of competition and the business end of the sport.

My pro career was cut short by a spinal cord injury that I received in my 3rd year at Dallas. I had "stingers" as a high school and college player, but as I matured the bone spurs that had developed on the upper portion of my spine had grown inward toward my spinal cord. I was unaware of this until my final play in football, which was a one-on-one pass protection drill with Ed "Too Tall" Jones in the summer of 1978 during Cowboy's training camp.

On this particular play, we were taking part in our daily ritual of one on one and two on two pass protection. These drills were always filmed from above so that we could review our techniques (feet, hand placements, knee bend, and explosiveness) in group film sessions. Upon contact Ed's feet left the ground and both of us fell backward on the ground. Ed got up following the play, but I did not. I had no feeling from my neck to my toes. As the feeling returned over the next few days, I was flown to Dallas for further testing and evaluation.

Charlsa: What direction did your career take following your injury? Can you identify the value of the lessons you learned as a player in regard to your development as a businessman, husband, and a dad?

**Jim:** When the neurologists determined that I shouldn't play the game anymore and I retired from football in Dallas, I went into commercial real estate as a broker. I called on property owners, and they would always want to talk about football or to see my Super Bowl XII Championship ring. After a month of that, I figured out that I was not getting any business done. So, I parked the ring in my safety deposit box and got back to business. I occasionally will bring the ring out for a special occasion, like a high school reunion, etc.

In a nutshell, athletics enhanced my natural tendency to take calculated risks and to apply commitment and resolve to stated objectives. It taught me to "look beyond hills" (impediments to progress), and that positive action is rarely taken in the local barbershop. As for my home, my wife and grown children would be the better judges of football's impact. I will say that I always have encouraged my wife and kids to pursue their own passions.

Charlsa: I would love to hear your thoughts on "conference re-alignment," scheduling and specifically losing traditional rivalries.

**Jim:** It's all about the $. The potential loss of regional rivalries is a tragedy. Can you imagine a day when Auburn and Alabama may not play in the last game of the season? I guess it is human nature to continue to tinker in an effort to stay competitive as a team, but some things are just better left the way they are. I long for the days of Johnny Unitas and his high top black football cleats. I saw Maryland's new uniforms the other day and sure didn't' like them. Collegiate and pro-football are redirecting their games to a different audience.

The day is coming when college football players will be paid (legally) for play. Billions of dollars are being generated, and it would seem a natural extension for competition to dictate that the best players will go the highest dollars (especially if regionalism dies).

Charlsa: Thank you so much, Jim.

## Roger M. Chapman, Alabama

Roger M. Chapman is a graduate of Morgan County High School in North Alabama. He played football at the University of Alabama where he was a "kick-off and field goal specialist." He received his degree in Geology from the University and has worked in that field since graduation. He and his wife, Amy have made their home and raised their children, Tyler and Caroline in Brewton, Alabama.

CAPTION: 2- COURTESY ROGER CHAPMAN, JR.

Roger is a respected member of his community, a leader in civic and church organizations and the University of Alabama Alumni and Athletic Department activities. In the midst of his numerous successes and accomplishments, he remains devoted to his faith, family, friends and…Alabama football.

Charlsa: I am interested in how you might compare today's big business of college athletics and the NCAA's role in it to your awareness of such things as a college athlete.

**Roger:** When I was in college in the mid to late 70's, nobody had a cell phone. You had the daily newspapers and TV news. But today, everybody's carrying a communication device. Any casual comment can immediately hit the airwaves. Today, we have entire networks dedicated to sports information. When I played, the NCAA's business didn't seem to receive as much attention. I believe the increased attention given to the "big time" programs today is the reason for the change. Competition is so key. More colleges are competing to recruit top athletes. The NCAA has to do a great deal more to stay on top of every institution.

Charlsa: What years did you play in the program there at Alabama?

**Roger:** I was a freshman in 1974 and graduated in August of '79. The easiest way to date my time there is that I was on the team that played Ohio State and Woody Hayes in the Super Dome in New Orleans and we won 35 to 6, and the following year, the famous "Goal Line Stand", when we beat Penn State in the Sugar Bowl for the National Championship.

Charlsa: The NCAA gives the appearance of having a lot more control over college athletic programs than in that period of time. Do you think there more rules and regulations today?

**Roger:** I think the NCAA's hand in things is like a big pendulum. Perhaps at times, they swing too far to one side and then back too far to the other side where it involves big time programs who are national contenders every year. Additionally, you have more college teams playing the game.

There's a great deal of money involved in games and TV contracts. NCAA rules are aimed at leveling the playing field and making the competition equal for the smaller programs. Compliance with so many rules can be tough, but I believe that schools do the best they can to keep their athletes and programs on target. At times though, we may go too far in trying to create a level playing field. In theory, it is great, but in practice, it may never exist.

Charlsa: Poorly thought out comments coupled with instantaneous communication can do more than cause trouble.

Ill-timed and thoughtless remarks can also bring a student athlete's NFL stock down. There is not a lot of room for error when you open your mouth these days as a player, so they must take great care with what is said.

**Roger:** I know the Universities go as far as they can to protect and to educate the players. Here's an example of what I'm talking about: Let's say I have a hunting cabin and I'd like to take friends hunting with me. Some of them are players, and some are not. How do you police these kinds of situations? As a fan or booster, you have to use common sense. In this case, it could be wrong to take a friend hunting and buy him things because it could be seen as an "athlete receiving improper benefits from a booster." Many have done these kinds of things with no intent to do harm or break a rule.

Charlsa: Since you played as a kicker, would you talk a little bit about changes that you see in special teams play?

**Roger:** Well I think the biggest change overall between now and the 70's and 80's, is the speed of the football game today. It is phenomenal. When I played, if you weighed 215 or 220, you were pretty big. Now you got people at 250 or 260 that can run like a deer. Special teams have to reflect his huge change. Bigger and faster players are needed to respond to the skilled people that catch and return the ball.

Still, you must stay in your lanes and make the play come to you. If you go chasing somebody that's got 4.1 or 4.2 speed, you'll end up running a big circle! They could be a world class sprinter, like Willie Gault. I kicked off to him once in a Tennessee game. I thought I had a pretty good angle on him, so I took off, but by the time I got to him, I was way behind him, and he went down the sideline to the end zone, untouched. There are Willie Gault-types in every game today.

As a kicker, you have to know whom to kick to and where to kick. Special teams practice schemes are designed to take away the kicking team's options. Special teams can change the momentum of the game in an instant. A hundred thousand fans are screaming because somebody breaks an 80-yard kick-off return. As a player, it can be difficult to regain composure after that.

Charlsa: It's interesting to me that I don't often hear much about outstanding kickers, or punters. In a recent magazine article, I noted that the "top" punters seem to average 45-46 yards a punt.

**Roger:** Well, in recent times we've seen the point of the kick-off change somewhat. We kicked from the 40-yd line. I used to get a few kicks 4 or 5 yards deep into the end zone, and there would be no return. Today, with kickoffs from the 35, the kicks are less likely to go into the end zone.

When punting, you want "hang time"- as much hang time in the air as possible to allow your coverage set-up downfield. If you kick a 55-yard punt with very little hang time, you've out kicked your coverage and "here they come" with a great return. So, you want to hang time on a punt that goes 40+ yards to allow time to set your coverage and stop the return.

Charlsa: I'd love to hear some stories about your personal experience if you don't mind.

**Roger:** One particular year, Auburn had 3 All-American running backs on a kick-off return. Cribbs, Brooks, and Andrews. On any given kick-off, they had those three guys deep: one back deep and one on either side. There was a "rule" that if there was a

TV timeout while a kicker was on the field, he was supposed to come off and talk to Coach Bryant, to put you at ease (like that would be possible!) Maybe you might tell a joke to relax while the commercial ran on the TV.

Once when we were playing at Legion Field, I saw the 3 All-Americans – Cribbs, Brooks, and Andrews deep. I remember asking Coach Bryant, *"Who should I kick it to?"* He said, *"Can you kick it over their heads?"* *"Yes sir,"* he said, *"that's what I want you to do. Don't kick it to any of them."* So, I put my mouthpiece in went back in.

I'd like to say I kicked it over their heads, but I really don't remember. Perhaps, Coach Bryant had a few other words in there that flavored it up a little, but I got the point!

On another occasion, we played Georgia at Bryant Denny, beating them by 9 points. I kicked 3 field goals and following one of these; I had a really nice kickoff. With a little wind at our backs, the ball jumped off the tip of my foot. It was just beautiful, floating end over end, deep into the end zone. I was half-way jogging down the field because I knew there wouldn't be a return.

All of a sudden from out of nowhere a Georgia player put his helmet right in my ear hole and knocked me completely to the ground. I got up kind of unsteady and was heading toward the sideline when he popped me and knocked me down again. I said, *"Hey man you're not going to return the ball, lighten up."* But by the time I said that he'd gotten me for the third time. When I finally got to the sideline, I said, *"I've got some kind of record here—knocked down three times on one kick off."*

It must have looked awful to the observer; it sure *felt* awful, and it looked even worse on the film Sunday afternoon! I learned my lesson though. My son played in high school, and my advice to him was, *"until the whistle blows, you'd better pay attention son, you might get hit from the blind side."*

We hear Coach Saban talk a lot about "The Process" and working until you are executing without mistake. Of course, these are 18-year-olds playing the game and they are going to make mistakes. Coach Bryant always said that if you make a mistake, make it full speed. I have no doubt that Coach Saban is absolutely the best coach we can have at the University.

Regardless of whether you played college football or not, the thing of pride is that you are attending THE University of Alabama – the flagship university in the state.

Of course, I have good friends who went to Auburn, too, and they feel the same way about Auburn. It was a great opportunity to be involved with the athletic program back in Coach Bryant's days there.

A day rarely passes without somebody saying, "Hey, this is Roger Chapman, he played at Alabama under Coach Bryant."

I'm just proud to be an alumnus like I know you are too.

Charlsa: I am! Thank you so much for taking time to talk with me and to share this on Southern Girls College Football Guide.

**Roger:** Well I hope it was helpful—you call anytime. And if you have questions, I'll do my best to answer them. Roll Tide!

## Dan Sartin, West Point

Dan Sartin is a 1974 graduate of Morgan County High in North Alabama and an Engineering graduate of the United States Military Academy at West Point. He served in the Army Infantry after graduation and had achieved the rank of Captain when he left the Army to enter the private sector. Dan did his post graduate studies at the University of Kansas, studying Engineering Management. The proud parent of two children, he now lives in Austin Texas.

At the age of 18, Danny's skill at football, coupled with his integrity, perseverance, and intelligence landed him an appointment to West Point. This is no run of the mill college experience; it takes so much more than most of us realize to succeed in such a disciplined and tough academic setting. His ability to adapt and flourish under these extraordinary requirements have served him well through the rigors of a military career and personal challenges. My admiration and respect for him and his accomplishments are immense!

Charlsa: Several of the boys you played high school ball with- including yourself, went on to play college football at various universities. That is unusual for small high school programs that would otherwise not be distinguished as "standouts" within the State. Do you have thoughts as to what characterized the teams and young men you played with in you high school career?

**Dan:** I think it is a combination of things. I remember summer vacations in high school when all we could think about was the start of football practice. It was an incredible mix of dreading the two-a-day practices, the anticipation of the first day in pads and getting to hit again, and just looking forward to that first game. The coaches encouraged us to prepare for the season, and all of us were focused on how we could improve. I think it is a feeling that continues to thrive in the south; football was such a big part of our lives. We lived for Friday night and game time. When I think of some of my fellow teammates and the accomplishments they achieved, I am so proud to be associated with them.

Charlsa: Tell us how you were recruited to play for and attend West Point. Were you expecting such an appointment?

**Dan:** I am still not sure exactly how it all transpired. I received a call one Friday night from a coach at West Point saying they had seen a film from our games in Hartselle and they wanted to invite me up to New York to try out for the Army Team. I went to West Point and tried out with players from all over the US and afterward I was asked to apply for admission to the Academy. I believe a MALO, (Military Academy Liaison Officer) submitted my name for consideration by the coaching staff. Military Academies rely on former grads to identify talent for admissions. I had to apply for nominations from my Senators and Congressmen for admission to West Point.

Charlsa: It's no secret that admission criteria at West Point are set extremely high. Your ability to play football was only one component of your acceptance. The character, personal tenacity and leadership abilities you possess played a huge role in being selected for study and training at our country's top military academy.

What positions did you play for Army? How does the size, weight, and speed of the game today compare with the years you played?

**Dan:** I started out playing defensive end for Army and then was moved to offensive tackle my sophomore year. I do remember being the smallest lineman on the offensive line, not a distinction I'm necessarily proud of! When I look at the players today, I am amazed at the size and speed they all possess. My size then would not even get me noticed in today's college football world.

Charlsa: I've heard other players make similar observations. Please give us a memorable moment from your playing days as a high school and college player.

Dan: In high school, it had to be key wins against our rivals (Decatur and Austin) and coming so close to making the state playoffs as a senior. In college, I cannot tell you how humbling it was to take the field for the annual Army-Navy game in Philadelphia.

At West Point, there is no game more important than the Army-Navy game. To see all of the former graduates, military heroes, and the immense display of patriotism in the stadium is something hard to describe and explain. Even today as I watch the annual game and see young athletes and future leaders of our military forces play a game with such tradition, knowing that they may well be in a war zone within a year of graduating, I feel a great sense of pride.

Charlsa: How has your experience at West Point and your military career served you as a businessman, a man, and a father?

**Dan:** West Point took the concept of teamwork we learned on the football field and ingrained in me the importance of that teamwork in all other facets of life. On the field and in the game the team's success depends on each member of the team doing his job to the best of his ability, supporting a common goal.

In the military, it may well mean the difference between life and death. The importance of teamwork in your family, your job, your life, it is the common goal that makes us successful.

Charlsa: Tell us a little about your Army career and then your business experiences since leaving the Army.

**Dan:** I served in the Army as an Infantry Officer assigned in Central Germany to the 3rd Armored Division. I was privileged to serve in various leadership positions and command a Mechanized Infantry Company on my first tour.

While in Germany I discovered rugby and was fortunate to play with The Frankfurt American Rugby Club. We played teams throughout Europe - an interesting transition from the full pads of football to no pads and full tackle rugby!

In the business world, I have worked with many great companies in the field of logistics and distribution.

Charlsa: Do you follow college football today?

**Dan:** Of course, college football will always be my favorite spectator sport. Whenever I can, I attend the Army-Navy game, and I also try to attend one game at West Point when possible.

I love the SEC and its dominance in college football.

Charlsa: Any parting comments that our readers might find interesting?

**Dan:** I just have to say that football in the small town of Hartselle, AL, literally opened up a world of possibilities for me.

Each Army football player passes a sign as they go out onto the playing field that features a quote by General of the Army George C. Marshall Chief of Staff during World War II. This sign says, *"I want an officer for a secret and dangerous mission. I want a West Point football player."*

I can assure you that every Army football player and officer takes that "charge" very seriously and aspires to that high calling.

Charlsa: Thank you so much, Danny.

Conclusion

# AS GOOD A STOPPING PLACE AS ANY...

I am hoping that this info will be a good starting point for the Southern Girls in all the "categories." Since we just scratched the surface here, we will be offering some more installments later on. I'd just like to suggest you watch a game or two and see if you can spot some of the "goings-on" mentioned.

Keep an eye open for the next editions and please, visit our Facebook Page, *Southern Girls College Football Guide*. Your questions and comments will be fuel for the fire and might even be featured in upcoming posts.

In the meantime, let me just thank you for taking the time to purchase and read this little book. I really love the idea that others are enjoying the game a little more as they learn a little more. So, go right ahead and demand equal time with the remote, prop your feet up on the coffee table and watch the college team of your choice!

Happy Football, Ladies!

Made in the USA
Lexington, KY
11 October 2017